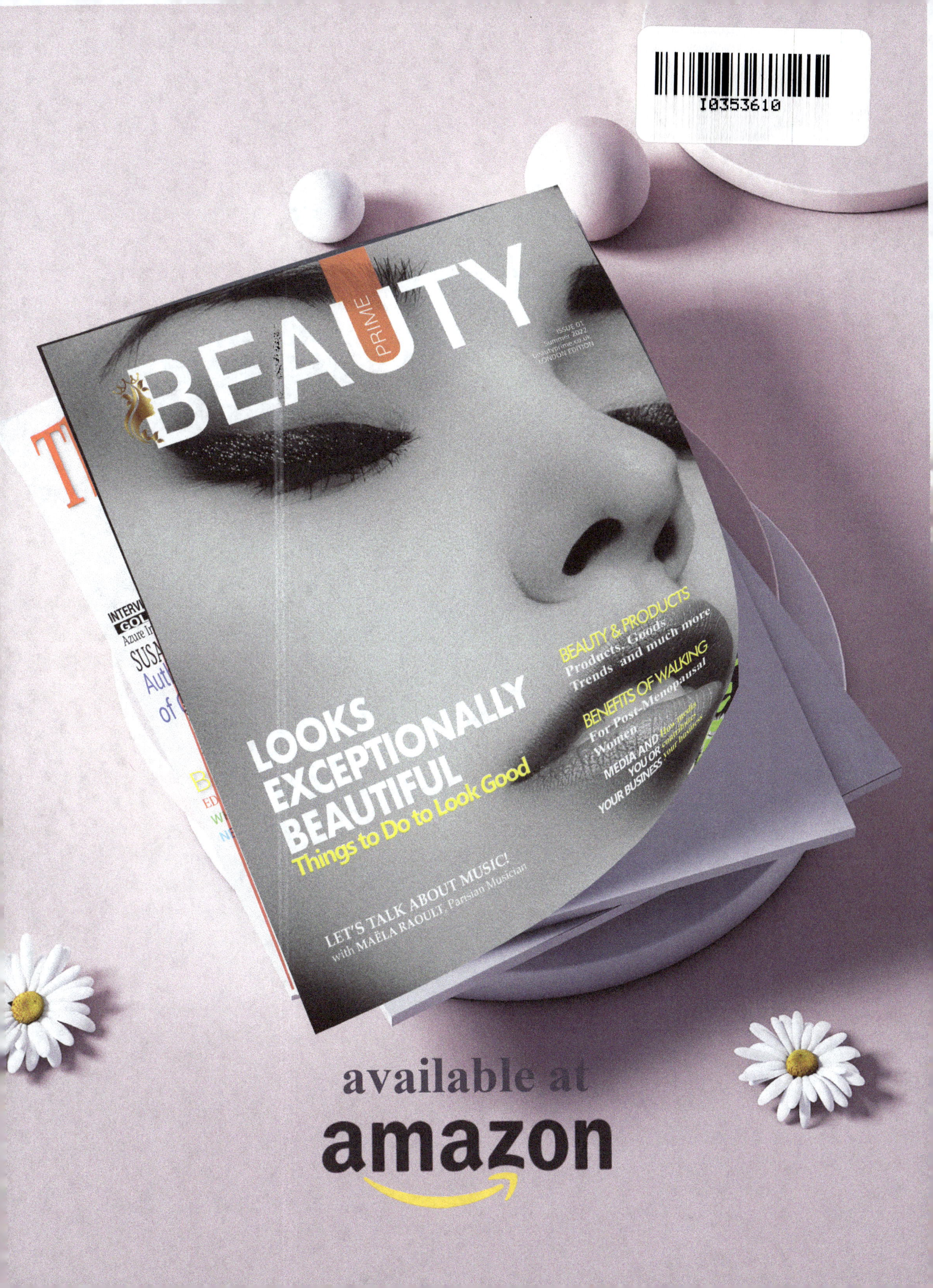

BEAUTY
PRIME
ISSUE 01
Summer 2022
beautyprime.co.uk
LONDON EDITION
BEAUTY & PRODUCTS
Products, Goods
Trends and much more
BENEFITS OF WALKING
For Post-Menopausal
Women
MEDIA AND How media
YOU OR contributes
YOUR BUSINESS your business
LOOKS
EXCEPTIONALLY
BEAUTIFUL
Things to Do to Look Good
LET'S TALK ABOUT MUSIC!
with MAËLA RAOULT, Partsian Musician
available at
amazon

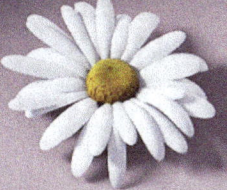

# Dive

## Into a Great Journey

Ready to
share
your
story?

**The Reader's House**
Make a phenomenal start
thereadershouse.co.uk

# IN THIS ISSUE

### 12
## MEDIA AND YOU OR YOUR BUSINESS

### 15
## FIVE QUESTIONS TO ASK YOUR WEDDING MAKEUP " ARTIST FIVE QUESTIONS TO ASK YOUR WEDDING MAKEUP " ARTIST

### 8
## ON THE COVER
*Looks Exceptionally Beautiful*

Having a healthy skin is essential for your looks. You will not be able to do much if your skin does not remain healthy as this is the foundation in which to build upon. It is the biggest organ in your body, so treat it well and drink lots of water.

### 17
## 5 AMAZING BENEFITS OF WALKING

### 20
## New Beauty Products

### 26
## HOW WOMEN ENTREPRENEURS CAN PLAN FOR SUCCESS

### 28
## INTERVIEW PRIME CLAIRE BARKER

### 29
## GET BACK IN YOUR FAVORITE JEANS WITH THESE WEIGHT LOSS TIPS

### 32
## How to Look Like a Top Model

### 38
## INTERVIEW PRIME MAËLA RAOULT

SCAN TO READ EMAG

# EDITOR'S LETTER

Welcome to First issue of Beauty Prime magazine that connects beauty stylists, make up artists, beauty salons, hair designers, and businesses in beauty industry. We bring them long form writings on different topics and unique interview, review and news subjects.

On the cover of this issue we feature a beautiful woman and the secrets of staying shape and astonishing. Suki tells why having a healthy skin is essential for your looks, and says that "You will not be able to do much if your skin does not remain healthy as this is the foundation in which to build upon. It is the biggest organ in your body, so treat it well and drink lots of water."

Beauty Prime is available both in electronic and print, over 190 countries and more than 40.000 online stores, retailers and libraries. It is available forever, and you can get it electronic or print from selected online stores including Amazon, Barnes & Noble, Waterstones, Blackwell's, Rakuten, Chapters&Indigo and so on.

In this issue; on page 12, Fatih Oncu wrote Media and You, or Your Business, explains how media contributes your business efforts. It is a prescription of yours including salon, barber and any other beauty industry business.

5 Amazing Benefits of Walking on page 17, Leslie C Smith tells you Benefits of Walking for post-menopausal women.

We have a section INTERVIEW PIME. In this section we'll feature Solon owners, beauty specialists, make up artists and people whom are in beauty industry.

Full of amazing stories, reviews, advice and news, you'll have so much fun with our new issue of Beauty Prime of this issue.

Enjoy reading...

Published by
Newyox Media
200 Suite
134-146 Curtain Road
EC2A 3AR London
t: +44 20 3695 0809
editor@beautyprime.co.uk
beautyprime.co.uk

*We are working remotely until further notice. Currently, we are still producing publications; should this change, we will contact any customers this affects. This means our phones have been turned off and we're currently only available by email (editor@beautyprime.co.uk) and whatsapp at +44 79 3847 8420. We will be answering emails as quickly as possible and we thank you in advance for your patience and understanding. We'll keep our website updated as and when things change.*

A. Harlowe
Editor
editor@beautyprime.co.uk
Dan Peters
Content Editor
dan.peters@beautyprime.co.uk

CONTRIBUTOS

Alexander Krivitskiy

Daniel Reche

Kanika Roberts

Kristina Polianskaia

Leslie C Smith

State Point

Pexels

Davide De Giovanni

COTTONBRO

Vinod Vullikanti

Shalini M

Suki Su

Rian Donatelli

Maela Raoult

*We assume no responsibility for unsolicited manuscripts or art materials provided from our contributors.*

# Looks Exceptionally Beautiful

*Having a healthy skin is essential for your looks. You will not be able to do much if your skin does not remain healthy as this is the foundation in which to build upon. It is the biggest organ in your body, so treat it well and drink lots of water.*

BY SUKI SU

The internet is full of beauty tips. However, there are some basic tips that can help you get started. The following 3 are a part of those tips, which will surely help you in getting the perfect look:

## Taking care of your skin

Having a healthy skin is essential for your looks. You will not be able to do much if your skin does not remain healthy as this is the foundation in which to build upon. It is the biggest organ in your body, so treat it well and drink lots of water. Yoou do not have to do much in order

PHOTO BY ALEXANDER-KRIVITSKIY

to maintain a healthy skin. You can get by with a few healthy habits and you will have the perfect skin. First of all, it is important that you provide your skin with the necessary nutrition. Then, you should ensure that you avoid any harmful habits which might damage your skin significantly, such as smoking.

Your skin requires a good supply of vitamin E and other minerals. For that, you should eat fruits and other natural sources of vitamins and minerals on a regular basis. You should figure out the type of skin you possess - dry, oily or normal. With this information, you will be able to find the right cream to apply on your skin. To avoid any harm on your skin, you should never forget to apply sunscreen when you go outside so you avoid sun damage and pigmentation issues.

## Maintaining a healthy lifestyle

Exercising and eating the right food is so important if you want to maintain good looks and stay youthful. Eating properly will ensure that your body gets the right nutrients. An unhealthy person does not look good and that it is a fact. Exercising will make sure that the nutrients you consume are used by your body too.

Having a healthy lifestyle will increase your self-confidence too. A high self-confidence will also help you look great because

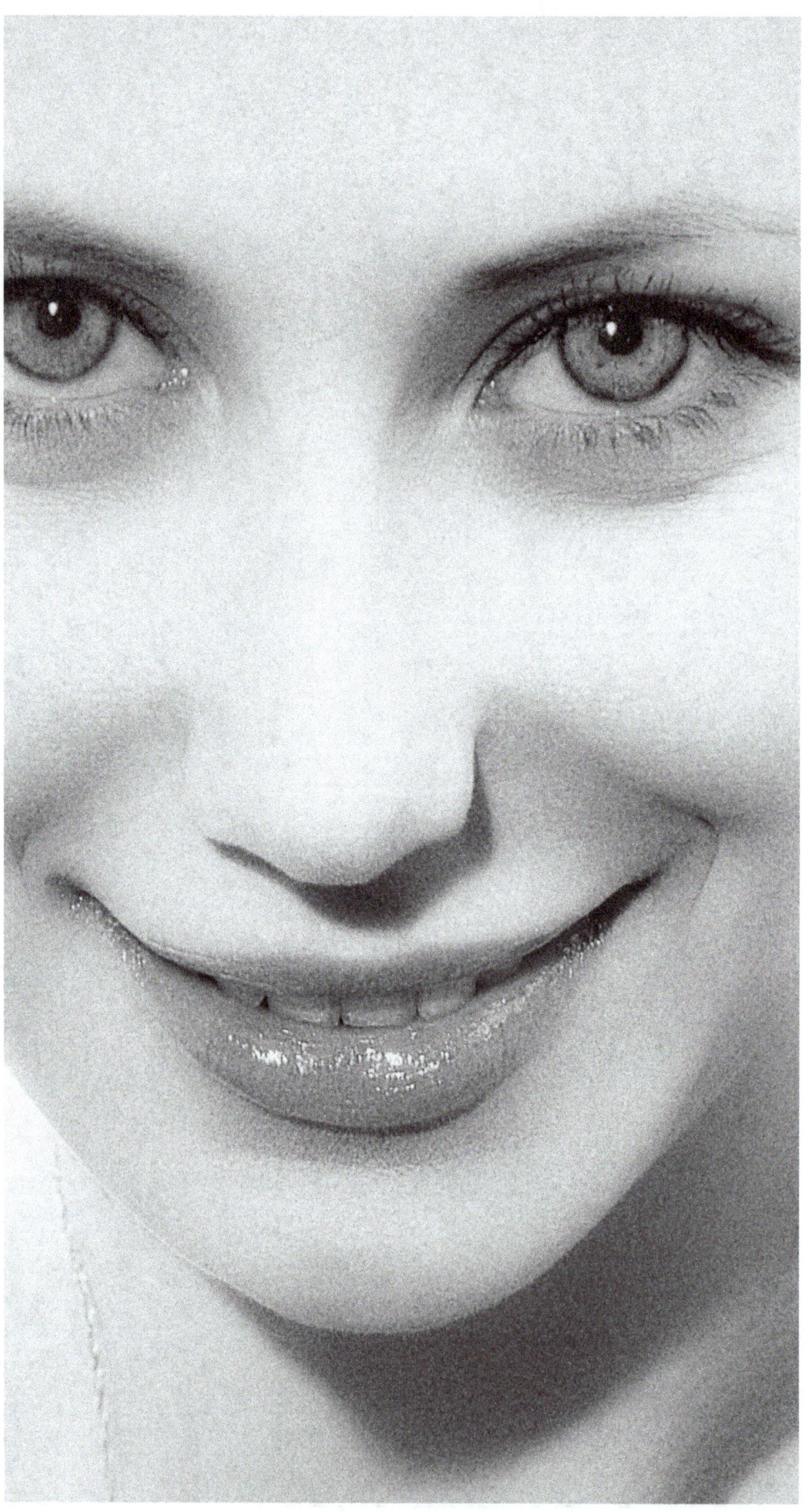

you will not have to act happy - your happiness will radiate. Confident people tend to look attractive easily and smiling in contagious ð

## Getting permanent makeup

Another major thing to do for your appearance is to get permanent makeup. Permanent makeup includes microblading eyebrows London or getting semi permanent eyebrows London based. You can choose to get permanent eyebrow tattoo London based or permanent eyeliner London based as well. With the help of permanent makeup, you will be able to remove the difficulty of applying makeup every morning.

You can find experts of this field without putting in much effort too. You can search for 'permanent eyebrow makeup near me' online. Most of the experts of this field are present online so you should not have any problems finding someone near you. Permanent makeup will give you perfect looks 24/7. The makeup will not get affected by water or sweat, so you can live life fully and free from any worries about running makeup.

## Conclusion

Out of all these points, the easiest thing to do is to get permanent makeup. It would be better if you begin with that. Apart from that, exercising and taking care of your skin will not be a hassle too once you get a hang of it.

Suki Su is an author of permanent-naturalmakeup.co.uk and expert for permanent makeup treatments. She offers the best permanent makeup, microblading in Rickmansworth, Watford, Pinner, North London, Central London, Harley Street. She has been writing articles on permanent eyebrow makeup near me for permanentnaturalmakeup.co.UK

SOURCE: Ezinearticles

# MEDIA AND YOU OR YOUR BUSINESS

*Media has been a powerful tool to influence people positively and negatively. Today, we live under the power of media as a source of information, communication and entertainment that enhance the knowledge of us through the different types of news or events in our daily lives.*

By F. ONCU
7 July 2022
London

LONDON - I involved either partly or directly many interviews with very successful Entrepreneurs. All these figures are the masters in their fields. I figure out something common in them; strong relations with the media. Ms. Emma, Heathcote-James, Founder/CEO Little Soap Company, Winner of Queen's Enterprise Award 2022, was one of them. I asked Emma what is the secret of her success comes? Her answer was remarkable; "I say Yes to Press! It doesn't matter what you are talking about – people will just remember you and the product. I would always say yes to news items."

Last month, when we decided to release a magazine, covers food and restaurant business, I decided to visit some restaurants in Royal Leamington Spa on a Tuesday evening, not a good day for most of the restaurants because it is either Monday or Tuesday. Yes, I was not wrong, almost all of them were no customers but one, Giggling Squid, a Thai Restaurant in Royal Priors Shopping Center on Recent Street. When I first see it from outside I thought there is something going on.

As I was walking towards the restaurant door with excited eyes, a waiter scratched me at the door. Please wait, she replied as soon as I said that I'm a journalist and would like to see the manager. Seconds later, he showed up outside of the restaurant and asked me how he can help me. As soon as I asked him what is going on here, and why the restaurant is full this evening, he replied; "We're like this almost every day. Of course, our course makes the difference yet the point is how we tell the people living in Leamington Spa and neighboring towns. Media is the solution. I do have all the contacts of media outlets in the town and around. We stay in touch with them and see them here most of the year. Sometime we get reviews and shares on social media. Publicity helps us to reach people here and around."

Media has been a powerful tool to influence people positively and negatively. Today, we live under the power of media as a source of information, communication and entertainment that enhance the knowledge of us through the different types of news or events in our daily lives.

It is a commination theory that "if you watch television more than two hours a day, your mentality would be televised mentality. You act and behave as you get form the television." This theory is told back to 50s. Today our mind is shaped by the tools of mass communication consist of television, radio, newspapers, magazines and internet such as : Facebook, Twitter, YouTube, Instagram, Google and other social networking channels. It simply means that media has the power to give information and provide an easy means of communication among people.

Media is a powerful and trusted tool among people living developed countries like the UK, US and EU. Here are some facts;

### FACTS ABOUT MEDIA

• 81% of consumers' purchasing decisions are influenced by their friends' social media posts. (Forbes)
• 66% of consumers have been inspired to purchase from a new brand after seeing media images from other consumers (Stackla)
• Consumers are 71% more likely to make a purchase based on media referrals. (Hubspot)
• Conversions increase 133% when

*You and/or your business have been a sourse of news, reviews and photos for media .*

❝Conversions increase 133% when mobile shoppers see positive reviews before buying. (Bazaarvoice)

> **81% of consumers' purchasing decisions are influenced by their friends' social media posts. (Forbes)**

### ABOUT THE AUTHOR

*Fatih Oncu is Founder and Director of Newyox, a London-based multi-sided media platform creates opportunities for publishers. He is also a publisher of a few magazines including The Reader's House, Entrepreneur Prime and London Taste.*

*He has over 20 years of experience in media, plus 10 years of education in Journalism at the College of Saint Rose (BA), Publishing at NYU (MS) and Digital Transformation at MIT (EP)*

mobile shoppers see positive reviews before buying. (Bazaarvoice)

- 78% of consumers say companies' media posts impact their purchases. (Forbes)
- 56% of consumers say they're more influenced by media images and videos when online shopping now than they were before the pandemic (Stackla)

### WHAT TO DO?

Depending on your business, lets say restaurant, there are many ways to make your food or items a news. You have a fancy restaurant, you're the only restaurant cooks and serves the steak, pizza and desserts. Yet many are not aware of it. Like many other businesses, restaurant business has parts. Media relation is one of them. Here are some of the things you should do;

*Web page.* Having an attractive, professional website is the best way to stand out from the competition. A good effective website helps build a strong online presence and helps communicate quality information to not just your consumers but media.

Make your webpage media friendly. Your webpage should have a "Press Room" page which should covers press releases, high quality images and recipes of some dishes you serve. Historical information about some of the dishes you have and news about people like political figures, artists, teams visited your restaurant. Reviews from customers and media should be in press room page as well.

*Press release.* Write a press release whenever find a reason like grand opening, seasonal opening, special dishes for special days like Christmas, Father's Day, Mothers Days, Valentina's Day or any new dishes you just started serving. The press release should include the atmosphere of your restaurant, lighting, location, ambiance and some of the reviews from costumers.

*Local Media.* Search and collect the list of any local media and contact the editors. Invite them to your restaurant for some reasons like press conference, introducing your new dish, or something about your restaurant contributes such as event, party or something like that.

*National Media.* Search and collect the list of national media, reviews restaurants and specializes in restaurant, food business. Contact The New York Times Restaurant Review editor if you are assertive about your cuisine, your services and the ambiance of your restaurant.

Stay with both local and national media editors in touch and send them press releases occasionally. They will eventually write a review or talk about your restaurant either on their media or social media.

*Reviews.* Be active on review sites, magazines and newspapers. As Bazaar Voice stated that conversions increase 133% when mobile shoppers see positive reviews before buying. Media reviews are most affective tools to bring costumers to your restaurant. Most customers read reviews before dining at the restaurant. So, reviews must be answered and managed. They can make or break your brand. Being proactive on reviews, both good and negative, is an excellent way to promote your restaurant.

*Grand opening.* Organize a grand opening all the time. If you open a new restaurant or branch that is a good opportunity to invite media, local political figures, artists and some of your loyal customers. If not a new restaurant or branch, do a season's opening, celebration or find a reason to invite these figures.

*Celebrate.* Celebrate your contacts birthday, holiday seasons, anniversaries etc. Send them a card or message. Invite them for a coffe or dessert.

*Get Awards.* Be an award-winning even be multi award-winning entrepreneur or company. There are many organizations willing to give awards. Register and be a member. There are also many events going on, join and get your awards. Than use these awards as a slogan when market your business; "Multi Award-Winning……"

*Social Media.* Social media is a part of mass media. Use and update them effectively. Social media has become the most influential and important virtual space where the platform is not only used for social networking but is also a great way of digitally advertising your brand and your products.

*Loyal Customers.* Don't neglect your loyal customers. Offer them something for free which could be tea, coffee, dessert and so on. They are ambassadors of your restaurant. Some of them may have contacts in media and some other channels.

*Build Your Media.* It's not just social media, it's a new media as well. Treath them you're the media patron and those are your media channels. Brotcast live events, news, conduct interviews through YouTube, Instagram and other channels. Build your own magazine. Newyox's state-of-art service enables people to get their own magazines with an affordable prices. The cost is low yet the effect is high. The magazines, Newyox creates, are available both print and electronic all over the globe in 190 countries and over 40.000 networks, platform, retailers and libries including Amazon, Barnes&Noble, Chapters&Indigo, Rakuten, Blackwell's, and Waterstones.

As a result, keep in touch with media is an essential part of your success not just in restaurant business but many other businesses. Whenever a new movie or a book released, they highlight what the media said. Whenever a new show starts, they highlight what media said. So, it's extremely important what media says about your restaurant, cuisine, desserts and ambiance.

The five main questions to ask your wedding makeup artist to decide if she's really "the one". If you do a little bit of prep work beforehand, your wedding day makeup artist would be one less thing to worry about.

PHOTO BY AMIR SEILSEPOUR

# FIVE QUESTIONS TO ASK YOUR **WEDDING MAKEUP ARTIST** TO KNOW IF SHE IS THE ONE

" So it's time to choose a wedding makeup artist. Doesn't it seem like there are a billion artists and a whole lot of pressure choosing the right one for your wedding? Well, this guide is the ultimate cheat sheet with five of the most critical questions to ask your potential wedding makeup artist before booking her.

BY KANIKA ROBERTS

**LIFESTYLE: MAKEUP**

**1 Have you ever done makeup on someone with my skin condition?**
At this point you probably already saw this makeup artists' portfolio of past brides or past work (which is why you are contacting her in the first place). However, what did those clients look like without the makeup? Did they have acne, black marks, scars, bags under their eyes, wrinkles, freckles, or a birthmark? You want to know that this artist can conceal and contour real faces with real skin conditions. Some before-and-after pictures may give you a clear idea if this makeup artist can handle your unique skin conditions. Because let's face it - a dab of lip gloss can make an already-beautiful model look even more fabulous, but a talented makeup artist can make her wrinkles disappear.

**2 What are your wedding makeup artist fees? (All of them.)**
How much is the total cost of wedding makeup services? Does that include a makeup trial? And how about taxes or gratuity? When do you pay? To whom? And how? Which types of payment methods are accepted? (Be wary if this makeup artist only deals with cash transactions.) Are there any hidden fees? Extra charges for extra services? Do you need to buy any products in advance? The answers to these questions will help you get a better idea of what you need to spend to get what you want on your wedding day. After all, you don't want to break your budget over unforeseen wedding beauty expenses.

**3 Do you have a service contract?**
Nowadays, you need to get specific details of your agreement in writing - even if your wedding makeup artist happens to be your brother's girlfriend's best friend. A clear outline of services could ease your fears and prevent any unpleasant surprises on your wedding day.

**4 Could I get a makeup trial?**
Of course you can, and you should! However, this question should really be, "how does the makeup trial work". You need to know how far in advanced could it be booked and how can you schedule one. At which location would the trial be? And who can you schedule it for? If you need a makeup trial for your maid of honor too, then you should ask this artist if she is willing to give you one. If she's not willing to be flexible, then this might be a deal breaker.

Wait - there's more. Have you stopped to think about who else may be at your makeup trial? Could friends or family attend your makeup trial? And on the flip side, who would this makeup artist bring with her to your wedding makeup trial? Beauty is important - but safety is first.

## 5 Would you be the same one who is doing my makeup on my wedding day?

This is HUGE! The last thing you need is to have Naomi do your wedding makeup trial and Jessica showing up on your wedding day to do your bridal makeup. Oh, hell no. That's a recipe for disaster.

The beautician who did your makeup trial should be the same one doing your wedding day makeup. Period. This is the only way you would know exactly what you are getting on your wedding day. Ask your wedding makeup artist if they will be working at any other event on your wedding day, and if so how many? Find out what would happen if your makeup artist have an emergency on your wedding day and cannot make the appointment.

So there you have it - the five main questions to ask your wedding makeup artist to decide if she's really "the one". If you do a little bit of prep work beforehand, your wedding day makeup artist would be one less thing to worry about.

Kanika Roberts and her team of professional makeup artists, are known as Face Candy Studio - The #1 International Carnival Makeup Company. It has been thriving for over 5 years and has become a major player in the New York Tri-State wedding beauty industry. Face Candy Studio makeup artists have now done over 1,500 makeup applications on carnival masqueraders and brides across 6 major cities. Specializing in bold, glamorous eye makeup and airbrush makeup, Face Candy Studio continues to draw loyal customers, and respect from within the Caribbean community.

PHOTO BY KRISTINA POLIANSKAIA

*NEED INSPIRATION FOR YOUR BIG DAY?*
Check out facecandystudio.com/weddings

# 5 AMAZING BENEFITS OF WALKING
## FOR POST-MENOPAUSAL WOMEN

BY LESLIE C SMITH

PHOTO BY DANIEL RECHE

Exercise is important for our overall fitness and wellness as we age. Aging can lead to mature women experiencing a decrease in muscle tone, flexibility and endurance. Exercise can help remedy these problems. However, many women don't exercise because it is often difficult to get to the gym, or they think the only way to do it effectively is to hire a personal trainer.

But, one of the most powerful exercises for mature women is something that is often forgotten when it comes to exercises; walking. Walking can be done anytime and it does not require any special training or equipment. In addition, walking has these 5 amazing benefits for post-menopausal women.

**Strengthens bones and joints**

As women go through menopause, they often lose bone density. This loss of density can result in osteoporosis, a condition that causes bones to be brittle and fragile. In our midlife years our joints also, suffer. After years of overuse, joints can become worn and achy. Walking, increases the blood flow to both bones and joints and thereby increases the amount of oxygen and nutrients to these areas. The result is bone density decreases and the joints are provided more support.

**Lowers blood pressure**

Hypertension becomes a problem for many women after they go through menopause. While blood pressure can often be controlled by the use of prescription drugs, walking has been shown as an additional way to reduce blood pressure. Brisk walking increases circulation, strengthens the heart, and thereby lowers blood pressure.

**Makes You Happier**

One of the more prevalent side effects of menopause for older women is depression and mood swings. This can be true even if these conditions were not a problem previously. Walking seems to help in this area by helping your body release endorphins. Endorphins are hormones which produce elation or an improvement in mood.

**Boosts Your Energy**

As we get older, our energy starts to wane. That easy two mile jog that you used to do every morning before work, now is taking more and more out of you to get it done. While you might not be able to do the run, you might be able to get in a brisk walk. A vigorous 30 minute walk can give you the energy to get through the rest of your day.

**Improves Your Immune Function**

Aging and menopause takes a toll on our bodies. More specifically, they weaken our immune systems. It becomes easier to catch colds, viruses, and other illnesses because our natural defenses are diminished. Studies have shown that walking in its overall effect, improves our immune function and helps us fight off illness. This is especially important if your ultimate goal is longevity.

*Walking has several benefits for mature post-menopausal women. It is an exercise that can be done, at your convenience or just as a part of your daily activities.*

As you can see, walking has several benefits for mature post-menopausal women. It is an exercise that can be done, at your convenience or just as a part of your daily activities. A caveat, however, is that to get the maximum benefit, you should walk briskly. You can start a vigorous walking program by yourself or get support by walking with friends. However, if you decide to make vigorous walking part of an exercise program, always check with your physician first.

Leslie Smith is a lifestyle strategist who believes it's not important how women grow old, but how we live young. For more tips on living your best life in your mature years visit her blog at [http://www.reinventinggrandma.com]

Source: EzineArticles

# Smart Flu Prevention Tips for Workplaces
## Experts aren't exactly sure what the upcoming flu season will look like

> "All employers should actively promote healthy habits to help prevent the spread of flu, address barriers, and make it easier for employees to get vaccinated at their earliest opportunity," says Albert Rizzo, M.D.

It's estimated that influenza sent up to 400,000 people to the hospital with flu complications and caused an estimated 22,000 deaths in the United States in the 2019-2020 flu season. As more Americans return to their workplaces, employers can play an important role in flu prevention.

While experts aren't exactly sure what the upcoming flu season will look like, relaxed COVID-19 preventative measures such as physical distancing, reduced travel, staying home and strict mask-wearing policies, will likely result in the return of seasonal flu. And because of a mild 2020-2021 influenza season, the 2021-2022 flu season may begin early and could be severe.

"All employers should actively promote healthy habits to help prevent the spread of flu, address barriers, and make it easier for employees to get vaccinated at their earliest opportunity," says Albert Rizzo, M.D., chief medical officer of the American Lung Association. "Keeping staff healthy benefits not only individual workers, but employers too, making flu prevention not only an obligation, but a smart business strategy."

As part of its Fend Off Flu campaign, the American Lung Association in partnership with Anthem Foundation is offering these tips to help businesses and organizations prevent the spread of flu and other illnesses in the workplace:

• Offer flexible paid sick leave policies to encourage employees who fall ill to recover without fear of lost wages.

• Offer telework policies that allow employees to stay home and care for sick family members.

• Advise employees to stay home if they feel ill. Individuals with the flu should stay home for at least four to five days after symptoms begin.

• Ask unwell employees to go home. Employees who appear to have flu symptoms at the workplace

PHOTO SOURCE: SouthWorks / iStock via Getty Images Plus

should be promptly separated from others and asked to recover at home.

• Provide facial tissue, no-touch trash cans, hand-washing stations, as well as alcohol-based hand sanitizer to promote preventive actions.

• Provide signage, such as posters and flyers, that explains healthy habits and employee policies.

• Help promote flu vaccination among your staff. Vaccination is the best way to help protect against the flu and over the course of over 50 years, hundreds of millions of Americans have safely received routine flu shots. Build vaccine confidence by addressing employees' questions and concerns and by sharing accurate scientific information and facts. Offer vaccination opportunities in the workplace or nearby in the community, as well as paid time off for vaccine appointments and recovery from illness. For more workplace flu prevention tips and insights, visit lung.org/fend-off-flu.

Influenza is a potentially serious disease that can lead to hospitalization, severe complications and death. Because people spend so much of their time in the workplace, employers have a special obligation and opportunity to help reduce employees' risk for contracting flu.

# New products
## BEAUTY

## First ever game-changing smart perfume

- This is the first 100-in-1 fragrance bottle controlled with an AI-powered App in the world
- Is the ultimate perfume PERSONALISATION…in the palm of your hand
- Has the highest quality fragrance
- Earth-friendly to reduce the 12 billion tonnes of plastic waste in the beauty industry
- Has a high-end Italian design
- Is reinventing fragrance as we know it

The founder of NINU, Marko Matijević, said they BELIEVE perfumes should follow your lifestyle and that wearing the same perfume every day and everywhere is like wearing the same pants every day to all occasions.

**What makes NINU smart?**

An AI-GUIDED app and an electronic micro-precision extracting system delivering every drop of the perfume is what makes NINU smart. It can precisely spray out each of the fragrances in different ratios and different volumes. The higher the volume settings, the more options you have. For instance, in the high-volume intensity, about 0,15ml of fragrance is sprayed out. NINU can deliver 120 different options!

With so many options to choose from - the days of half-full bottles becoming dust collectors are over. Instead of getting bored with a fragrance, NINU allows you to turn the formula upside down and create new mixes to keep things fresh.

If you do not know what fragrance to wear, just let NINU use her Artificial Intelligence (AI) enhancement to suggest certain scents to fit your current day and mood. It tracks your scent tendencies, time of day, and the weather outside.

Extensive efforts helped in designing a premium perfume bottle and assembling the best tech. The heart and soul of NINU reside in its fragrances. We entrusted this incredible challenge to a master perfume team led by the talented Dominique Moellhausen. Dominique's dedication to the art and admirable contributions in the industry awarded her "Perfumer of the Year" at the 2020 Beautyworld Middle East Awards.

## SODA Makeup and Disney's Frozen II collaborate on magical new makeup collection

- *SODA Makeup announces latest collaborations with Disney's Frozen II and The Little Mermaid.*
- *The cruelty free brand aims to inspire creativity in a safe, non-judgemental zone.*
- *#exploretheocean and #showyourself with these magical new ranges.*

The latest collaboration between SODA Makeup and Disney's hit franchise, Frozen II brings a whole new meaning to the phrase 'perfect match'!

Together with the love and magic of Disney, SODA has created two stunning works of art in their latest collections: Frozen II and The Little Mermaid. Brought to life using the highest quality products, these sparkling ranges will help you along on your creative makeup adventures. Travel to the golden, autumn leaf-speckled forests of Arendelle with Anna. Then, you'll land up among the white-capped mountains of Elsa's Winter Castle, with cool-toned snowflake-inspired shades fit for an ice queen! The Frozen II range comprises a selection of pressed and liquid highlighters; a highly-pigmented eyeshadow palette, featuring both warm and cool tones; pressed shimmers and volumizing mascara, among other products.

Then, take your journey deep beneath the ocean's surface in Ariel's underwater kingdom, with a wide, colorful selection of shades, textures and pigments fit to help you #exploretheocean. Featuring a rosy liquid cheek stain, long-wearing eye pencils, glittery lip gloss and a face palette, this underwater range is bound to tick all your boxes!

The products are designed to uplift the wearer, allowing you to fly high among the rainbow-tinted skies. SODA's warm embrace of creativity offers a safe zone where you can showcase your artistic experimentation to the world.

As bright and eye-catching as their adjacent films, and long-lasting as an ancient kingdom, these Disney collections aim to inspire you to #showyourself through the art and beauty of makeup.

# New products
## BEAUTY

## Pioneering skin tag remover TagBand surpasses one million sales after device goes viral

TagBand devices have been designed to remove skin tags via ligation - making a formerly troublesome treatment affordable, accessible and simple.

TagBand has surpassed one million sales after developing and popularizing a pioneering skin tag removal device.

The game-changing product utilizes the removal method known as ligation by applying silicone bands around the base of skin tags. Ligation means to restrict blood supply which is vital to a skin tag's growth and survival.

Despite 46% of American adults suffering from skin tags, treatments have traditionally been restricted to invasive freezing or burning procedures.

With skin tag removal often not covered by health insurance policies, sufferers have even resorted to home methods - such as cutting off growths with nail scissors.

But TagBand devices have provided a non-invasive and budget-friendly solution to a prevalent health issue. Sales have hit seven figures since the brand launched in 2015 - cementing TagBands' status as a market leader.

Videos on TagBand have helped send the brand name viral; one instructional YouTube upload has been watched more than 7.7 million times, whilst a user review has attracted over 9 million views. The product is also widely seen on television - with a commercial running on US networks in 2021.

TagBand devices are available in two kits and two sizes to target specific types of skin tags. Both the 'Original TagBand' and 'Auto TagBand' devices work in the same way - but are applied slightly differently. The more affordable Original TagBand requires two-handed application (suitable for skin tags in easy-to-reach areas like the neck), whereas the Auto TagBand is designed for one-handed use for more elusive skin tags.

Devices come with 10 rubber bands included - capable of treating up to 10 separate skin tags.

## Eneschi CBD bath bombs that can relieve anxiety, improve sleep and soothe skin

NaturallyCBD is home to one of the UK's best collections of infused bath bombs bursting with health benefits

Nottinghamshire based NaturallyCBD has launched a brand new line of Eneschi branded CBD and Essential Oil infused bath bombs, bursting with physical and mental health benefits.

The cannabidiol company has added to their selection of luxury bath bombs, to complement its growing itinerary of natural health remedies, giving customers the chance to take advantage of CBD's power and bring spa like treatments to their bathroom.

NaturallyCBD's new bath bombs come in various colours and scents, with the presence of cannabidiol - extracted from the hemp plant - guaranteeing a relaxing, soothing soak that leaves skin feeling refreshed and rejuvenated.

Loaded with Essential Oils for their hydrating, anti-bacterial, and antifungal properties - which can improve skin conditions - NaturallyCBD's bath bombs also provide welcome relief from general aches and pains whilst easing symptoms of anxiety and improving sleep overall.

Alongside the range of bath bombs and cbd skincare items designed to protect skin and prevent breakouts, NaturallyCBD also has a sports range with products offering muscle repair benefits for faster recovery.

Hair care serums are available online, too, with CBD balancing the scalp's natural sebum levels and resolving issues such as dryness, flaking and dandruff.

A NaturallyCBD spokesperson explained: "The best thing about CBD is that it's not for any one person - everyone can benefit.

"Whether it's older people wanting to relax with a bath bomb or a member of the younger generation hoping to recover from a sports injury, there is a product here that can help."

# New products
## BEAUTY

## New Natural Enzyme mask with Medical Grade power to exfoliate and resurface your skin

Hedox Clinic is excited to announce its new OhMySkin Sublime Enzyme Face Mask. The unique, natural, enzyme-based clinical formula dissolves the protein bonds between dead skin cells and new skin cells, enabling the dead cells to shed and fresh new skin to be revealed, thus delivering outstanding and immediate results. After just one application your skin will look and feel distinctively different.

The radiance-boosting mask contains a myriad of potent botanicals including; Cactus Enzyme, Wheat Grass Extract, Meadowfoam, Moringa Oil and a range of concentrated vitamins, all of which also have powerful antioxidant, anti-inflammatory and anti-bacterial properties.

Packed full of effective, natural ingredients, OhMySkin includes no harsh acids, abrasives or micro beads, which can burn, scratch and irritate the skin surface and lead to premature aging. The mask uses innovative enzyme technology to gently exfoliate the skin by removing the dead skin cells and resurfaces the skin by revealing the newly formed, fresh skin beneath. The mask is great for even sensitive skin and delivers fantastic clinical-level results; clearing and refining pores, rejuvenating the skin and brightens the complexion.

"What we really love most about the OhMySkin mask is the effectiveness, yet gentleness of the natural ingredients. After just the first use, your face feels so clean and smooth!" Comments Dr Humble, Medical Director for Hedox Clinic and OhMySkin. "OhMySkin is as effective as a chemical peel, but without any of the burning and inflammation. Plus, it is a fraction of the cost and you can do it in the comfort of your own home." Dr Humble added.

**The benefits of OhMySkin Sublime Enzyme Mask:**
• Refinement - Blocked pores are revealed and cleansed, reducing their size.
• Resurface - Surface is left scrupulously clean, smoothed and polished.
• Lifted - Skin is rejuvenated with a pleasant, uplifted sensation.
• Cell Renewal - Our actives are proven to increase cell renewal, essential for a fresh, vibrant complexion.
• Perfecting - The appearance of scars and blemishes improves with regular use.

## Brides Flock Abroad As National Wedding Costs Soar!

With the lingering presence of our favourite virus, 2021 finally sees the easing of lockdown rules limiting UK wedding ceremonies. UK wedding costs have spiked following the lifting of restrictions, standing at an average of £27,161. This figure is ever rising. Staycation honeymoons are also considerably more expensive than their foreign equivalents, with rates of self-catered accommodation in the UK soaring to 41% above equivalent prices in 2019.

Cliphair conducted a survey to delve deeper into the effects of COVID on attitudes to weddings in 2021. Over 50% of all women asked said they would prefer to have a wedding abroad in 2021, a stark increase from the 25% in 2019.

The alarming staycation rates also appear to drive newlyweds out of the country for their honeymoons. Again, when asked if they'd prefer to travel abroad or remain local, 86% of women preferred to brave restrictions for overseas Covid honeymoons.

# New products
## BEAUTY

## Woman-Owned Brand VANNA Releases Collaboration With Alana Hadid

## Manchester skincare and haircare brand grüum launches range of wash bags made from ocean-bound plastic

Inspired by her father's love for watches, Alana Hadid's entrance into the watch world was inevitable. But it was her fondness for VANNA that turned her ambitions into reality. "I love what VANNA is doing. They're bringing the ability to be a watch collector to those who don't have hundreds of thousands of dollars. People want something that's high quality and beautiful without breaking the bank", says Alana.

Her affinity for watches materialized after receiving an heirloom from her father: a rare, vintage double-faced watch from the 1930's.

"My family were refugees. That's a small piece of my family. The watch was more concealable jewelry so it was easier to get out. My grandfather gave it to my father and he gave it to me."

A story as old as time, watches have held family history for hundreds of years and are often passed down through generations. Typically a male-dominated industry, Alana was drawn to VANNA as the only woman-owned and woman-manufactured watch brand.

"The designs are innovative but finding out VANNA is a female founded company was incredible. And this is really coming full circle, because I hope, later on, I can pass my VANNA watch to my daughter", reveals Alana.

In collaboration with Alana, VANNA has released 100 limited edition and numbered watches. The dial of this watch is made of natural Tiger's Eye, Mother of Pearl and features a Sapphire crystal. A stone of protection, Tiger's Eye may also bring good luck to the wearer. It has the power to focus the mind, promoting mental clarity, assisting us to resolve problems objectively and unclouded by emotions.

Nacre, also known as mother of pearl, is an organic composite material produced by some mollusks as an inner shell layer; it is also the material of which pearls are composed. It is strong, resilient, and iridescent. Mother-of-pearl shell is commonly believed to attract prosperity.

Known as the "wisdom stone", Sapphire releases mental tension, depression, unwanted thoughts and spiritual confusion.

A new range of wash bags made from ocean-bound plastic has been launched by grüum, the Manchester-based skincare and haircare brand.

The loop Wash Bag, which is available in three colours, is ethically sourced and 100% vegan.

Each bag is made from 100% recycled plastic pellets derived from ocean-bound plastic - such as plastic bottles, plastic fishing nets and flip flops - that has been rescued from the seas or intercepted before it reached the shoreline. Each contains the equivalent of up to 12 plastic bottles.

The new range comes as non-profit organisation Plastic Oceans estimates that 10 million tonnes of plastic is dumped into our oceans every year, the equivalent of a truck-load every minute.

Sustainability is a key principle at grüum, which was launched by four friends from Manchester in 2016 and has doubled sales in the last year and grown to 20 staff.

Co-founder Andy Shaw said: "Sustainability is at the heart of everything we do. From our ever expanding range of zero-plastic products to our packaging choices, it's really important to us."

Originally starting out as a shaving brand, grüum has now expanded into skincare, haircare and suncare products that, in its words, are "kind to skin and our planet".

Inspired by Scandinavian ideals, all grüum's products - which are mostly manufactured in England - are free from chemical "nasties", the company said, and packed with natural ingredients.

Shaw said he and his co-founders - Simon Leonard, Beth Sleigh and George Lagonikas - had given up their jobs and launched the company in a bid to challenge the status quo in the beauty industry.

He added: "We only want to create products that serve a real purpose, with no gimmicks or labels. Sustainability and inclusivity are core pillars of everything we do, so we don't make things 'for him' or 'for her'; we make them for everyone, with one fair price for all."

# New products
## BEAUTY

## 2021 Home-Making Wedding Gifts from Bedsure Home

## Haryali London Expands Its Product Line And Goes Multilingual

Haryali London, thanks to the success it has earned in the past few years, has decided to expand its product range and bring the consumers more grooming and shaving items. The company is known for its vast and high quality range of hair care and other grooming products and brings to you varied brands and product types. In the past one year, the sales of the company have gone more than double and this has encouraged them to bring more brands and products for its happy and satisfied customers.

The creative team as well as the owners of the brand, Haryali London felt a need to meet the growing needs of the customers and the only way to do so was to introduce a wide variety of more grooming and hair care items. Each product being introduced has been thoroughly researched upon and studied to make sure consumers only find satisfactory items whenever they log onto this online portal. Besides this, the company has also gone multilingual by launching the site in its German version. Haryali London is also planning to roll out more languages including Italian, French, and others for its website. This is another way of meeting global customer needs and being more accessible to people with different language backgrounds.

These recent developments are nothing but further proof of the fact that Haryali London is fast becoming popular and is trying to grab the global markets. In today's scenario where people prefer buying everything they need through the web, hair care and grooming products too have a huge scope online. Haryali London has perfectly banked on this trend and brought grooming from physical stores to their web store. The web traffic it receives has touched high numbers and making full use of this, the owners decided to roll out a new product range at the right time. If one has to predict a forecast for the company's future, it shall surely be an increase in revenue in the new fiscal year.

Research shows that late summer and autumn are the most popular times of year for couples to get married in the UK. As home-making gifts are popular for newlyweds, Bedsure has identified 5 wedding gifts that are suitable for nuptials in the UK in 2021.

Many newlyweds want gifts to make their house a home, including bedding and other products. Bedsure has a range of suitable gifts to help those planning to attend a wedding. The company has a range of products to make people's homes and bedrooms comfortable, cozy and relaxing.

**Satin Pillowcases**
Satin is a popular fabric for those who desire comfort and softness. The Bedsure Satin Pillowcase Set has been voted as 'Amazon's Choice' for 'satin pillowcase' and has over 22,000 global ratings. The two-piece set features polyester satin with envelope closure to keep the pillow from sliding out. Available in 13 colours, Bedsure Satin Pillowcases can match with a wide variety of bedroom décor.

**100% Cotton Waffle Weave Blanket**
This lightweight blanket is suitable for relaxing at home on a couch, taking evening walks and getting that extra bit of warmth in bed. Bedsure's 100% Cotton Waffle Weave Blanket features wrinkle-resistant and classic-looking waffle weave, and is available in blue, gray and dark gray. Customers say this Bedsure Blanket is ideal for summer, doesn't need to be ironed, is soft and keeps its shape.

Marble **Pattern** Microfiber Bedding Set
For couples that like a luxurious look, Bedsure Home's Marble Pattern Bedding Set works well. Available in gray, black or white, this duvet cover pattern is reminiscent of a classic mansion or luxury hotel. The 100% brushed microfiber fabric provides softness and smoothness.

**Memory Foam Mattress Topper**
For newlyweds that have all the home décor and bedding they need, yet complain about back or spine problems when sleeping, the Bedsure Home Memory Foam Mattress Topper makes a great gift. Featuring 7 cm of head, neck, back and leg support, this mattress topper also features a non-slip bottom and a washable, zipped cover. Bedsure's Memory Foam Mattress Topper has achieved 'Amazon's Choice' for 'double bed memory foam topper.'

## New products
### BEAUTY

## Merohealthcare introduces "Award Winning Premium Beauty Products" from Now Foods

Merohealthcare, registered in the name of Web Health Company Pvt. Ltd. is a newly established private Online Pharmacy in Nepal which is dedicated to providing fast, reliable and cost effective healthcare products and/ or services.

Recently, Merohealthcare introduced 5 premium beauty products manufactured in USA by Now Foods. Some of these skincare products have won international award in their category. They guarantee to provide several health benefits. These award winning skincare products are listed below:

1) Vitamin C & Sea Buckthorn Moisturizer
2) Vitamin C & Sea Buckthorn Lotion
3) Charcoal Detox Facial Mask
4) Blemish Clear Spot Treatment
5) Glutathione Skin Brightener Cream

These premium beauty products are Paraben Free, Gluten Free, Cruelty Free and Vegan/ Vegetarian.

The company is presenting these products at a flat 15% discount as an introductory offer. Visit their website www.merohealthcare.com to know more about these products.

Merohealthcare is a fast growing online pharmacy, an online medical drug store to buy medicines, healthcare products, beauty essentials and surgical & healthcare devices in Kathmandu, Nepal. It is a complete online healthcare service provider with free* home delivery service and has been operating since December of 2019.

## Natur'Alley introduces the most exciting plant-based Face Balm on the Market!

A must have for any skincare routine, this new face balm crafted by Natur'Alley will leave your skin feeling soft and velvety, with no greasy residue. Perfect for daytime use as part of your skincare routine, this stunning face balm can also be used overnight as a repairing mask for a flawless facial skin.

Take a few minutes to treat yourself and simply massage this fresh Rosemary & Palmarosa formula into your face, then all that is left to do is sit back and let our face balm do all the hard work. Its natural ingredients have been specifically selected by Natur'Alley for their recognized health properties which help in the reduction of fine lines and blemishes and give the skin a more plump appearance.

This wonder balm was crafted using a unique blend of natural butters enriched with Rosemary essential oil which will help lightens dark spots and blemishes resulting in an improved facial skin complexion. The anti-inflammatory properties of this wondrous essential oil will also help to reduce swelling and puffiness, heal burns and soothe the skin. Furthermore, Natur'Alley went even further and paired this formula with Palmarosa essential oils which will balance the smegma production in the skin to help maintain oil levels. With its antibacterial properties, Palmarosa essential Oil is excellent for treating oily, acne-prone skin.

This face balm is perfect for use daily as part of your skincare routine, but also overnight to repair, protect and maintain a glowing and healthy facial skin thanks to its astonishing anti aging properties. The new Natur'Alley face balm is mostly recommended for dry skin complexion, and can also be used as a terrific overnight face mask which will leave your facial skin plumped, conditioned and fulsome in the morning.

# HOW WOMEN ENTREPRENEURS CAN PLAN FOR SUCCESS

The nearly 13 million small businesses owned by women nationwide are essential to the U.S. economy. Accounting for 42% of U.S. small businesses, they employ nearly 9.4 million people and generate $1.9 trillion in revenue annually.

Healthy and growing women-owned businesses are vital to an inclusive economic recovery, yet women entrepreneurs face distinct challenges, including fewer resources and less access to professional networks, on top of having a greater share of caregiving duties.

"For many small businesses, having access to trusted experts in areas like marketing, business planning, technology and legal can be a critical turning point for getting back to growth," says Jenny Flores, head of Small Business Growth Philanthropy at Wells Fargo. Right now, the company is deploying over $55 million from its Open for Business Fund to 93 nonprofits across the country to provide more women and diverse entrepreneurs with resources.

According to Flores, these tips and resources can help entrepreneurs pivot from surviving to thriving as they recover from the pandemic and look to the future:

### MENTORSHIP

Connecting with mentors is a powerful way for women business owners to share best practices and learn from each other but it's often hard to know where to find them or initiate those relationships. A new program between Wells Fargo and the Nasdaq Entrepreneurial Center called Connect to More is giving women entrepreneurs complimentary support through its signature Milestone Mapping Coaching Circle. Born from the challenges of COVID-19, participants get hands-on help setting and reaching business goals from a network of peer mentors and industry experts.

"As a non-profit committed to access and equity in entrepreneurship, we are grateful to partner with Wells Fargo to help women business owners accelerate their personal and professional growth as leaders and gain support as they solve big problems that make their families and communities stronger," says Nicola Corzine, executive director, Nasdaq Entrepreneurial Center.

### NETWORKING

Networking is more than a buzzword. It can help open doors to growth. Check the local chamber of commerce or consider joining a well-known organization like the National Association of Women Business Owners.

### KNOWLEDGE

Knowledge is power. Visit Wells Fargo's Women-Owned Business Resources page for free tools to support critical business decisions. Also, female entrepreneurs should check out some of these women-specific podcasts to pick up new strategies from savvy leaders:

• Being Boss digs into the mindsets and tactics that can help women business owners make money doing what they love.

• She Leads features respected female leaders from all industries who let listeners know what it takes to rise to the top.

• The Center offers a playlist of workshops and classes for women-identifying entrepreneurs.

• Women at Work, hosted by Harvard Business Review editorial staff, features conversations about where women are and how they can move forward.

### STRATEGY

Having a concrete business plan is essential to running a successful business. During the pandemic, many small businesses had to create more online offerings, change relationships with supply chains or reduce hiring. Now's the time to review which of these adaptions can be built upon in the future.

Running a business is never easy. But new resources and support can help women entrepreneurs overcome the distinct challenges they face and plan for growth as the economy picks up.

(StatePoint)

# HOW TO MAKE A HYBRID WORKFORCE SUCCESSFUL

With metrics for COVID-19 improving, many companies are starting to consider returning to work in person. But most employees and employers agree it won't look like it did before.

Indeed, research shows a large chunk of companies today are sizing their physical offices down, as more people work from home all the time or part of the week. And hybrid offices, arrangements where team members are in two or three days a week and work remotely the rest of the time, seem to be the wave of the future.

However, experts say that business owners and managers should not approach hybrid offices the same way they do completely remote set-ups.

"While there are very specific benefits to hybrid offices, they come with their own set of challenges," says Michele Havner, director of marketing at Eturi, the maker of Motiv, a recently-introduced app that small- and mid-sized business owners are using to improve productivity.

Motiv is a mobile dashboard that delivers important productivity metrics to CEOs, managers and leaders. The tool's reporting focuses on providing conference call activity and email summaries and integrates with Google Workspace and Microsoft 365, with many additional integrations and features slated for future release. Havner says that such tools function as a virtual corner office vantage point, helping to smooth out communication, collaboration and workflow issues created by hybrid arrangements and decentralized workspaces.

Equally important to communication is simply being mindful that hybrid offices can cause challenging dynamics among team members. Taking steps to address those issues preemptively can save headaches down the line. This includes making everyone accountable for meeting goals and deadlines. It might also mean offering the same perks to in-office and work-from-home staffers, while giving those who come into a centralized workspace the same level of flexibility remote work affords.

Easily adopted by small- and medium-sized businesses, which have been underserved by existing productivity solutions, Motiv is available through the iOS App Store and Google Play Store. To learn more, visit motivapp.com.

While hybrid offices can ultimately reduce costs and help keep employees healthy and safe, business owners will need to stay flexible and keep their workforce focused. Leveraging tools that facilitate hybrid work situations will be a key to success for companies as they move forward.

StatePoint

PHOTO BY DRAZEN ZIGIC / ISTOCK VIA GETTY IMAGES PLUS

INDEED, RESEARCH SHOWS A LARGE CHUNK OF COMPANIES TODAY ARE SIZING THEIR PHYSICAL OFFICES DOWN, AS MORE PEOPLE WORK FROM HOME ALL THE TIME OR PART OF THE WEEK.

## INTERVIEW PRIME

# NEVER FAIL, LEARN FROM THE EXPERT

## CLAIRE BARKER
### Business Growth Coach

"I'm naturally suspicious of programmes promising great things but 18 months with an EC Coach has shown me that what Nige and his team deliver is every bit as good as they promise. I just wish it had existed 25 years ago when I started out.

Having expert help 'on-tap' when you need it has been amazing and helped me get so much done. We've made massive progress and I'm well on-track now to get the business to where I want it to be…"

JAMES WRIGHT DOUBLE RED PHOTOGRAPHY

### What coach training have you attended?

I was a Business Analyst and Project Manager for 10 years and loved my job. Following a company takeover I was made redundant.

So I joined my husband's business doing the admin.

What I quickly realised, running a business you need to know every department. I started on a long path to find ways to make our business run efficiently without breaking the bank.

I took many wrong turns but when I found Entrepreneurs Circle I knew I had my answers.

I became a member and got ways to effectively implement positive results in a no nonsense way.

Within a few months they approached me to see if I would be interested in becoming a self employed certified coach and I jumped at the opportunity.

The training and support I get helps my clients achieve more and get the lifestyle they want.

*To date, we've upsold £16,425 worth of business to our own list - without spending a penny to find new customers. Genius!"*

**NICK ASH WILL AND PROBATE SERVICES**

### What size business do you specialize in coaching?

I specialise in small businesses of 100 employees or less. Though the main reason for having a mentor is being open to change and the hard work that's needed to succeed.

### What industries have you coached?

I have coached a variety of industries but that's what makes it exciting.

### What do you do best? What someone does best is not the same as that in which they specialize.

Life gets in the way sometimes but having someone who can give you techniques and support to keep the business going is vital support. Even on a daily basis you need to ensure you are utilising the day to its full advantage.

### What additional skills besides coaching do you bring into play?

I bring my analytical skills that allows us to look at business improvements and make savings and more efficiency.

I also offer my productivity knowledge as I've had to learn to do more in less time and I live with illnesses.

I understand what's it like to run a business and how to avoid the pitfalls.

To me that's a unique combination to get businesses succeeding.

# GET BACK IN YOUR FAVORITE JEANS WITH THESE WEIGHT LOSS TIPS

- Eat Smart and Often
- Keep the Good Stuff Where You Can See it
- Don't Go It Alone
- Find Your Routine and Stick With it

*Do you have a favorite pair of jeans sitting in your closet with the hopes that one day they will fit again? You're not alone!*

American women want to lose an average of 16.8 pounds to fit into their favorite pair of jeans and nearly 39 percent say they like to keep jeans in their closet that don't fit to motivate them to lose weight, according to a survey by Nutrisystem.

And while trying on jeans that don't fit from the back of your closet or even a new pair at the store can be frustrating, being equipped with the right tips can help you get on the weight loss track and back in those jeans.

PHOTO BY DAVIDE DE GIOVANNI

PHOTO BY COTTONBRO

### EAT SMART AND OFTEN

Aim to eat smaller meals every two to three hours, six times a day so that you don't binge or overdo it. You'll feel full and satisfied, which will help you make smarter choices.

### KEEP THE GOOD STUFF WHERE YOU CAN SEE IT

It may sound overly simple but it's true, you are more likely to eat healthy foods if you put them in a visible, easy-to-reach location. And for the fridge? Don't put your fruits and veggies in the produce bin! The middle shelf is the sweet spot. That's where to keep your celery, carrots, apples, oranges and all that good stuff.

### DON'T GO IT ALONE

Losing weight isn't exactly a cake-walk. But it doesn't have to be impossible. Find a weight loss plan that works for you and fits in with your lifestyle. Programs like Nutrisystem ensure you feel satisfied throughout the day and take the guesswork out of dieting, making it easier to stick with the plan and drop those pounds.

### DRINK UP. HUNGER AND THIRST ARE EASILY CONFUSED, SO STAY HYDRATED

But don't make the mistake of drinking your calories," says Courtney McCormick, dietitian at Nutrisystem. Opt for water. If you're looking for a more flavorful option, add fresh fruit slices, a few squeezes of lemon or some sprigs of mint leaves.

## FIND YOUR ROUTINE AND STICK WITH IT

It's important to make a plan for what you'll eat and when you'll exercise each week. Carve out part of your day that works for your schedule and you'll be much more likely to follow through.

You owe it to yourself to focus on your health. Making changes is never easy at first, but hang in there. Your results will fuel your continued commitment. (StatePoint)

Remember, making healthy changes can help you solve your denim dilemma and get you back into your favorite jeans in no time!

# How to Look Like a Top Model

The best and the most direct way of becoming a model is to join a modeling agency. Modeling agencies have many different clients, and therefore they are able to provide you the best clients and assignments that suit your needs.

By Vinod Vullikanti

odeling is perceived as if it is a representation or a "certification" of superiority in appearance because not everyone can become a model. Being a model impresses people and because of this, there are actually many people who will light up at the thought of being a model. As such, this article will be to help those who aspire to be a model, but do not know how to get started.

1) Know the kind of model you want to become

There are various forms of models, from runway models to commercial models, event models, blogs-hop models, photo models et cetera. People tend to generalize the term "models", meaning they associate models solely as runway models, which is obviously not the case. You need to know what kind of model you want to become before you set your sights to becoming one. For example, if you are tall, have sharp facial features and a slim body, you might want to try to be a runway model. If you are good at socializing and grooming yourself, you can try out event modeling. There are many different options, but be sure to find out which one suits you best.

2) Finding a modeling agency

In order to kick start your career in modeling, there are various different ways. Like promoting yourself on social media, blog posts and even joining competitions. However, the best and the most direct way of becoming a model is to join a modeling agency. Modeling agencies have many different clients, and therefore they are able to provide you the best clients and assignments that suit your needs. However, most modeling agencies will require you to pay a premium, which can range from hundreds to thousands of dollars. The money paid will be used to create a portfolio, which includes having professional photographers take photos of you and creating a composite card. The modeling agencies will then send your composite card to clients who will then review and see if you are suitable to be their model for their project. The main thing to note is, while all agencies will have their own client base, not all agencies have many clients. Meaning to say, you have to do your research and find out the agencies which have many different clients. That way, it increases your chance of securing projects, otherwise, you could be left in the cold after paying the fee.

3) Understand the trend of modeling

The modeling industry is not very huge, though it is getting better. Unfortunately, not everyone can make it big by simply modeling. Meaning to say, you should not rely solely on modeling to earn a living. Yes, it could be a path to joining showbiz like Mediacorp, but it is not very common. In the world, Caucasians are preferred to Asians for modeling. They are generally taller or have better features and proportions, while Asians cannot really hold a candle beside them. Of course I am not saying for everyone, hope you do not misunderstand.

All in all, if you dare to dream, dare to try out, you stand a chance. You never know what will happen if you do not try. Do your research, get your mind and body ready, like grooming yourself and maintaining a healthy diet, and you will realize that your dream is not far away.

Wondering how to get into modeling? Getting Started as a Model. iModels Holdings is the leading model agency in Singapore.

Source: http://EzineArticles.com/9388082

# Eleven Smart Ways To Make New Friends

BY SHALINI M

If you are looking for smart ways to make friends with new people, you are on the right page. In this article, we have shared several smart tips that can help you make new friends. Read on.

## 1. Get in Touch with Friends of Friends

Typically, people share common interests with friends of friends. So, you can ask your friends about their friends. Reach out to them to see if it works out. And in most cases, it does work for most people.

## 2. Organize a Meet-Up

You can organize a local or online "meet up" with individuals who have similar interests as you. It's a good idea to join an online friendship club as well.

## 3. Borrow a Dog

If you have a pet dog, you can take it to a nearby dog park. There you may be able to make friends with other dog owners. You can also borrow a dog if you don't have one already.

## 4. Go to a New City

Although it may be a bit intimidating to go to a new city on your own, you should try it. You can get a good book, sit in a park and wait for someone to approach you. Alternatively, you can also get to someone and start a conversation.

*If you are an office worker, you can have lunch with your co-workers. It will give you plenty of time to spend with your colleagues. Maybe you can make friends with some of them.*

## 5. Spend Time with Co-Workers

If you are an office worker, you can have lunch with your co-workers. It will give you plenty of time to spend with your colleagues. Maybe you can make friends with some of them.

## 6. Try Adult Leagues

In many cities, you have adult leagues that may help you get in touch with like-minded people. But if you are not into team sports, you can join a yoga studio or gym. Regular visits can help you meet many familiar faces.

## 7. Visit a Local Supper Club

You can pay a visit to a nearby Supper Club with the hope to see new people. At these clubs, you can eat, drink and make friends with the type of people you like the most.

## 8. Take Pictures

If you like taking tons of pictures at a party or event, you can make friends with many people. All you need to do is ask them if they are on Facebook. This way you can send them the photos they like and make friends with them in the process.

## 9. Attend Cultural Events

Usually, attending cultural events is free. For instance, you can attend an art exhibit, concert or play.

## 10. Open Up

When you talk to a like-minded person, make sure you open up to them. This is important to build trust and make a stronger bond of friendship.

## 11. Be a Volunteer

It's a good idea to offer your help or services as a volunteer. This will help you make new friends while contributing to the community.

So, if you are thinking of making new friends, we suggest that you try out the tips given in this article. This will help you get rid of your boredom and spend quality time with good friends.

Datting India offers a great way to help people make new friends. If you want to make friends with new people, you can join a Friendship Club in Bhopal.

*(EzineArticles)*

# SkinPro Celebrates Launch of Men's Facial Cream 'The Daily Wingman'

*The Miami-based skincare company continues expansion with the launch of its first product in the booming men's skincare sector.*

For more information, visit SkinPro.com

Men of all ages and races fall victim to environmental factors such as UV rays and pollution on a daily basis. It's also inevitable that men can develop poor skin complexion, and even adult acne, simply from being healthy and active. To add insult to injury, celebrating success in life and doing "guy stuff" like staying out late, consuming alcohol, and smoking cigars leads to eye bags and unsightly dark under-eye circles. The end result is the look of a beaten, downtrodden man each and every morning.

Nobody understands this constant battle more than SkinPro Founder & CEO Tim Schmidt, who describes himself as "an obsessive soccer Dad who when time permits explores the world, collects tequila, and will never turn down a round of golf or a fine cigar." Schmidt has worn many hats for the global skincare brand over the years, and along the way has been highly involved in all states of product development, perhaps most importantly personally testing each concept for efficacy.

A demanding work and family life coupled with the scorching Florida sun taught Schmidt early on just how important a skincare routine was.

"Life often moves at a pace that doesn't allow a lot of time for self-care. As a man who fully understands this, I've created an easy-to-use facial cream for men that is not only easy to use but affordable for men of any stage in life," said Schmidt.

The Daily Wingman Formula aims to add swagger and confidence to men of all ages and races. Formulated with DEFENSIL®, a skin conditioning agent that soothes skin, calms inflammation, and remedies redness, this product is what the active male needs to stand out in any competitive environment.

Natural extracts from organic green tea, in addition to oils derived from avocado, coconut, olive, lavender, and peppermint protect the skin's surface from oxidative damage caused by free radicals and environmental stressors such as pollution and UV rays. Within days of being listed on Amazon.com, the product launch was discussed on blogs catering to men such as JustLuxe, ManTripping, UnfinishedMan, and MenWhoBlog.

Early reviews are positive, and the company expects this to become a flagship product that helps create more awareness to the importance of skincare for men.

Small Business

# 8 TIPS

# Eight Tips to Prepare
## FOR A VIRTUAL INTERVIEW

With these tips you will be well on your way to not only acing that interview, but job offers galore! Break a leg and most of all, be yourself, and let your personality shine!

### BY RIAN DONATELLI

**First and foremost,** it is still a "real" interview, and should be treated as such. There is a person on the other end who will be making an executive decision about your qualifications for the job, so assume it's no different than if you met this individual in person.

**Dress to impress!** Even if they won't see your feet, dressing from head to toe in at least business casual attire is the first way to not only look professional when the camera goes live, but help you get into the right mindset. You'll be surprised how you will feel you can take on the world when you LOOK like you can!

**Find a quiet and professional location for the interview.** If you have a home office, this is perfect. If not, most libraries offer conference rooms free of charge, which you can reserve for yourself for the duration of the interview. There is nothing less professional than children, pets, or other household distractions infringing on your interview experience, and greatly affecting your appearance of professionalism. If you cannot get away from the home, set up a a dining room table or in a living room, and make sure everyone in the home knows you need some privacy for the allotted amount of time.

**Try out the interview system in question before the interview.** The day or night before, log on and familiarize yourself if it's a program you've never used. Even if it is something you use often, like FaceTime, double check that you have the contact info correct.

**Pay close attention to the time zone the interviews are conducted in.** This one is SO important. With the advent of virtual interviews, corporations have opened themselves up to a huge network of individuals all over the world, and while advantageous, also likely means they operate on a different time zone than yourself. No one wants to get off on a bad foot because you missed your interview or were late because you were

PHOTO BY POLINA ZIMMERMAN

unsure of the time zone. If it isn't clarified anywhere in a confirmation of any kind, reach out to your recruiter or interviewer, they will be happy to give you the information, and glad that you were proactive.

**Try to use a laptop or desktop if at all possible,** but if you have to use a Smartphone, set up a tripod system beforehand, so your hands can be free for the interview. You can even use a stack of books. What you don't want to do is hold the phone for the duration of the interview; this is a professional encounter, not a FaceTime chat with your grandma.

**Like any interview**, make sure you have studied up on the company and position you wish to hold. Google them. See if they have had any news lately. Did they recently merge with anyone? Or perhaps they made a branding change not long ago. In the very least, know the goods and/or services they offer, and be prepared to tell them how you could aid them in this niche if you were hired.

**Prepare questions.** Almost always the interviewer will ask you if you have any questions, and if they have answered all of them, its fine to tell them so. However, this is your chance to have their undivided attention, and ESPECIALLY if you are offered a job directly following. You will want to have compiled a list of anything you might have wanted to know, rather than bombarding the interviewer's inbox with emails less than 24 hours after they had time set aside to make themselves available just for you.

With these tips you will be well on your way to not only acing that interview, but job offers galore! Break a leg and most of all, be yourself, and let your personality shine!

Co-Author Colette Pfeiffer Talent Booking Experts & Connections Consulting and Marketing Solutions team.

**INTERVIEW PRIME**

# LET'S TALK ABOUT MUSIC!

## MAËLA RAOULT
### Parisian Musician

*Curious about all musical worlds, she studied improvisation and jazz with great personalities of Parisian Jazz.*

*Born in Brest in 1990, Maëla obtained her Musical Diplomas at the Conservatories of Brest, Paris and Brussels. Passionate about chamber music, she plays in various formations at many events and festivals : Origami, Courant d'air (Brussels), Préludes à l'orchestre de Paris (salle Pleyel), Tout sauf Debussy (CRR Paris), Les Harmonies (Billiers), Concerts at the university campus of Paris…*

### How did you first get into music?

I had health problems as a child (rheumatisms). I couldn't do sport very often and was slowed by pains and cramps.

So my mother proposed me to play an instrument. I started in the town where I was born : Saint Renan in Brittany. I played music in the bands of every surrounding villages.

Music was also important to my godfather. He was a renowned English teacher in Brest. He arrived in France at 20 after theological studies. He lived in Tulles before settling to Brest. His mother was a famous singer in Northern Ireland.

Then I went to the conservatory in Brest. Music was a passion for me. I had the chance to begin to play in professional orchestras with my teachers at 14.

I was good at school, particularly in sciences. I preferred literature but it was too complicated for me. The passion for people, the desire to discover new musical styles, and new cities were bigger. I was good at my instrument and I wanted to play in a classical orchestra as a professional.

I left Brest in 2008 to study and enhance my technical skills and musical culture at the Paris conservatory. I also spent two years in Brussels.

### Where do you see your musical career in 10 years?

I don't know where I will be in 10 years. I'm more concerned about the present.

I spent few years teaching and playing in Paris. I'd like to leave now. I'd like to travel and see other countries. I'm a concertist. I'm first of all a classical chamber music player and a contemporary music specialist. I'd like to meet new people, collaborate with new orchestras and ensembles.

Other styles of music are also important to me. I like to improvise in all styles of music. From swing and be bop to world and pop music.

I compose sometimes and have many songs for jazz quartet or quintet ready to record but my first job is to be a performer. That's the reason why I wanted to become a musician.

Pedagogy is also very important to me. I've written, arranged and transcribed 3 books for young clarinet players. It's a collection named The French Touch' Collection. I also like to give masterclasses and work with young students.

### What would you say is your greatest strength as an artist?

I think it is to be connected to the present and open-minded. Today you have to be connected to other branches of work. You have to develop your technical and mental skills and have a minimum of competences and knowledges in every domain. You have to give your best everyday.

### Who is your favorite musician?

My favorite musician is Wynton Marsalis.

### What is your proudest accomplishment as a musician?

My new album Reflections could be my proudest accomplishment. I like to create music. To play living composers music, to find a way to serve and generate my best in accordance with the composer's will and creativity.

### What interests or hobbies do you have outside of music?

I go to the swimming pool and do yoga quite everyday. It keeps me in good health, helps me refraining my rheumatisms and maintaining a good instrumental technique.

Photography is another passion. It's another actual way to express myself.

During the summer I also like to go sailing with my brothers and father. We crossed the channel many times.

# 5 Household Cleaning Hacks Using Essential Oils

*For clean, healthy, bug-free spaces, consider introducing essential oils into your home's supply kit. A small but mighty dose can go a long way.*

(StatePoint)

From cleaners and sprays to air fresheners and more, essential oils are making their way into the mainstream as commonplace, common sense household solutions.

It's no surprise then that the market for essential oils is anticipated to grow significantly (more than 9 percent) over the next several years, according to Grand View Research. More households are catching onto the fact that these beneficial plant-based ingredients have a range of cleaning and home care uses.

To get in on the trend, consider these cool home care uses for essential oils:

• Wipe Surfaces: Creating your own cleaning supplies can make chores a little easier on the eyes, nose and throat. The good news is that certain essential oils, like tea tree and lemon oil can help fight dirt and grime, as well as kill bacteria and viruses, making them an excellent addition to homemade cleaning solutions and wipes.

• Banish Bugs: Most traditional home insecticide products use the same active ingredients initially developed almost 50 years ago. Interestingly, the right mix of essential oils can also be highly lethal to bugs. Familiar ingredients such as lemongrass oil and geraniol in Zevo Instant Action Sprays target nerve receptors active only in insects, not people or pets.

"Zevo bug sprays are effective because they target insects' unique biology with a blend of effective essential oils, setting them apart from traditional insecticide sprays," says John Scarchilli of Procter & Gamble Ventures, which sell Zevo online and at select Target and The Home Depot stores.

• Bust Fridge Odors: Even if you regularly rid your fridge of old items and wipe down its surfaces, combatting fridge odor can be a losing battle, as the plastic components tend to absorb odors over time. Make that box of baking soda that you have in your refrigerator work a bit harder. To go beyond simply neutralizing odors, add a few drops of essential lemon oil to it for a crisp, fresh scent.

• Revive Fabrics: Take a natural approach to fresh-smelling fabrics. Create your own spray by combining baking soda, distilled water and a touch of your favorite essential oils. Use the formula on linens, upholsteries, window treatments or any other fabrics around your home in need of a scent boost.

• Create Calm: You don't have to do a full hygge-inspired renovation project to promote a peaceful atmosphere in your home's spaces. With just a diffuser and such essential oils as lavender and bergamot, you can fill a room with a calming scent.

For clean, healthy, bug-free spaces, consider introducing essential oils into your home's supply kit. A small but mighty dose can go a long way.

# BEAUTY PRIME

*Looks Exceptionally Beautiful*
**Things to Do to Look Good**

**Beauty & More**
Products, Goods Trends and much more

*Let's talk about Music*
with MAËLA RAOULT, Parisian Musician

**Benefits of Walking**
For Post-Menopausal Women

MEDIA AND Busy media
YOU OR contributes
YOUR BUSINESS your business

---

**Beauty Prime** magazines are available print, flip and electronic in 190 countries. Our magazines reache more then 40.000 retailers (including Amazon, Barnes & Noble Waterstones, Blackwells, Rakuten and local independent bookstores in the United States.)

Visit beautyprime.co.uk for more.

# YES! I would like a subscription to Beauty Prime

- ☐ Current Issue for $ 19.99   ☐ Includes Shipping and Handling
- ☐ One-Year Subscription ( __6__ Issues) for $109.99
- ☐ Two-Year Subscription ( __12__ Issues) for $199.99

☐ I am a renewing a current subscription        ☐ I am a new subscriber

Name: _____        Phone: _____
Shipping Address: _____
Billing Address: _____
Email: _____

☐ Yes, I would like to receive updates, newsletters and special offers
☐ No, I would NOT like to receive updates, newsletters and special offers

**Payment Type:**   ☐ Cash     ☐ Check     ☐ Credit Card

Card Number: _____
Card Holder: _____   Exp. Date: _____

Please mail this form to:
**Magazine Name:**   200 Suite, 134-146 Curtain Road EC2A 3AR London

Beauty Prime by Newyox                                    beautyprime.co.uk

**Subscribe Now!**